BITTERGIRL

BittERGiRL

ANNABEL FitzsimMoNs

ALisoN LAWRENCE

MARY FRANCiS MOORE

bittergirl
first published 2009 by
Scirocco Drama
An imprint of J. Gordon Shillingford Publishing Inc.
© 2009 Annabel Fitzsimmons, Alison Lawrence, Mary Francis Moore

Scirocco Drama Editor: Glenda MacFarlane
Cover design by Terry Gallagher/Doowah Design Inc.
Author photo by Rachael McCaig
Printed and bound in Canada on 100% post-consumer recycled paper.

We acknowledge the financial support of the Manitoba Arts Council, The Canada Council for the Arts and the Government of Canada through the Book Publishing Industry Development Program (BPIDP) for our publishing program.

Library and Archives Canada Cataloguing in Publication

Fitzsimmons, Annabel, 1971-
    Bittergirl / Annabel Fitzsimmons, Alison Lawrence, Mary Francis Moore.

A play.
ISBN 978-1-897289-38-9

I. Lawrence, Alison, 1959- II. Moore, Mary Francis, 1969- III. Title.

PS8611.I897B48 2009   C812'.6   C2009-901773-3

J. Gordon Shillingford Publishing
P.O. Box 86, RPO Corydon Avenue, Winnipeg, MB Canada R3M 3S3

Thanks to our bitterboys: director and dramaturge Michael Waller; designer and stage manager John Patrick Robichaud; our first "D" Stephen Reich; and later David Macniven who picked up where Stephen left off. Thanks as always to our families for their support, and thank you to Glenda MacFarlane and Gord Shilllingford.

(l to r): Mary Francis Moore, Alison Lawrence, and Annabel Fitzsimmons

Annabel Fitzsimmons survived the public humiliation of being dumped in a restaurant by learning to wrap her legs around her head and becoming one of Toronto's busiest yoga teachers. She is a freelance writer and a much sought-after health and fitness consultant.

Tired of re-enacting her break-up with her daughter's Ken and Barbie, broken-down single mum **Alison Lawrence** found salvation in a pair of strappy sandals, a well-shaken martini and by creating *bittergirl* with Annabel and Mary Francis. A writer and actor, Alison's other plays include *And All For Love* and *The Catering Queen*.

Mary Francis Moore is an accomplished actor, director and writer who has worked across Canada, in the US and England. She was given the Twelve Vegetables of Christmas by one hapless ex but eventually got over him by having the entire German National Volleyball Team over for a swim.

Bitter? You bet. But they got over it by joining forces and writing *bittergirl*, the play, publishing the self-help book *Bittergirl: Getting Over Getting Dumped* and dispensing relationship advice all over North America in print and on radio and TV, including NBC's *The Today Show*, CBC Radio One's *Sounds Like Canada*, *Glamour* and *Elle*. *bittergirl: the musical* is currently in development. Success really is the best revenge.

Cast

Production Credits

A twenty-minute version of *bittergirl* was first produced at the Rhubarb! Festival at Buddies in Bad Times Theatre, Toronto, in 1999 with the following cast:

A.. Mary Francis Moore

B .... Annabel Griffiths

C ....Alison Lawrence

D... Stephen Reich

Directed by Michael Waller
Stage managed and designed by John Patrick Robichaud

The first full-length production of the play was produced by the bittergirl co-op at the Tim Simms Playhouse, Toronto with the same cast, director, stage management and designer in November of 2000.

Scenes

Franco's

Three women, sitting onstage, waiting, at a small café table. D, a man, enters, carrying three bouquets of roses. He produces them with a shy flourish. The women gasp with pleasure, smell them appreciatively and begin to speak.

A,B,C: We are sitting in our favourite

B: Saturday night

C: restaurant

A: he and I

B: him and me

C: us

A,B,C: having some

A: wine:

B: Caber—

C: net Sauvignon—

A: Out of our usual price range.

B: Franco brings us our

C: appetizers

A,B,C: Hi Franco! *(They wave.)*

C: We share

A: oysters on the half

B: shell and artichoke

C: hearts. He plays with the stem of his glass,

A: sexy,

B: his watch reflects off the

C: knife—he's wearing the blue

A: sweater, the one I made him!

B: He's so handsome—I

C: look up and he's got that

A: little boy

C: half

B: smile

A: What?

B: I say,

A: You've been acting strange all day, he's

C: got that faraway look—

A: What are you thinking

B: about—this morning?

D: No.

A: Do you

C: have something

B: to ask me? He clears his throat.

D clears his throat.

D: I don't know how to do this…

B: Oh

C: come

A: on

B: just

C: do

A: it!

D: You know how much you mean to me…

A,B,C: And… *(Repeat ad lib: and, and, and.)*

D: but…

A,B,C: But… *(Repeat ad lib: but, but, but.)*

D: We need to talk. It's too soon it's too much I feel trapped…

            The women speak simultaneously with D as he speaks.

A: …I'm instantly nauseous…

C: …I can't see…

B: …everything is in slow motion…

D: …I need to be alone I'm a mess I'm a really shitty person…

A: …I'm sweating…

C: …everything sounds muffled…

B: …I have an oyster stuck in my throat…

D: …this hurts me so much I wish I wasn't the one leaving you're too good for me…

A: …my mind is racing…

C: …I'm going to throw up…

B: …was it the sex?…

D: …you deserve better than this I can't give you what you need. *(Alone, after B's last line.)* I love you I'm just not in love with you.

C: …this isn't happening…

B: …does everyone else know?…

A: …is there another woman?…

D: *(Alone, after A's final line.)* …you will always be my best friend.

A: Franco arrives with our main course.

A,B,C: Hi Franco…

B: Linguini

A: Arabietta with

C: shaved parmesan…

A,B,C: Yum.

A: No words.

B: Just wine.

C: Sobs.

D: Are you alright?

A,B,C: I'm fine! *(Big, bright smiles.)*

A: The restaurant is very quiet.

B: People are staring…

C: I'm convulsing.

         The women start to shake with silent sobs.

D: Maybe I should go—

         The women lunge at him with outstretched arms.

A: NO DON'T—

C: GO DON'T—

B: LEAVE ME!

            He leaves.

C: Franco turns the music up.

D: *(He turns around.)* I'll call you.

            The women watch him walk away.

A,B,C: Franco brings me the check!

            *A beat, then they burst into three heaving sobs, after
            which the lights snap down.*

I Have to Go

            C alone onstage.

C: So I'm touching him, y'know, just touching him?
            And he's been away and now he's back and we
            haven't, well, done anything for how long? and
            suddenly he stiffens, just stiffens and says—

            From a distance.

D: I have to go.

C: Go where? To the bathroom? To the kitchen? To the
            theatre? To his mum's? France? Go eat? Go pee? Go
            do something? Go build a house, fly a kite, write a
            play, eat a meal? GO WHERE?

            Closer.

D: I have to go.

C: Yeah, well, I have to go too. I have to go DO some
            things, some big things, some important things... I
            have to go finish my law degree, produce a movie,

no, that'd be a film, I have to write that novel, paint that painting, run that corporation, I have to sit on the Supreme Court I have to BE someone really important in the cultural life of our country… No, I have to go, go pick up our child at daycare, go cook our dinner, go do our laundry, go organize your life, pay the mortgage, do my taxes, cut her toenails, clean the lint out of the dryer… Where?

Now onstage with her.

D: What do you mean where?

C: What do I mean, I mean where do you have to go?

They speak together, ending at the same time face to face.

D: Somewhere. I have to go Somewhere. Somewhere, where I can get some space. Where I can be alone. This is killing me. This life is crushing me. I'm losing myself. As an artist. As myself. I don't know who I am anymore. I think I need to be alone. Just alone. Just myself.	C: Somewhere. He has to go Somewhere, anywhere but here. Somewhere where he can be alone. We are killing him. This child and I are crushing him. Squeezing the lifeblood way the hell out of him.

A breath, then they speak together again.

D: The more I love you and the child the less I have of myself.

C: The more I love you and the child the more of myself there is.

And they speak together again.

D: The more I take on the more paralyzed I become.

C: The more I take on the more I am capable of. *(Pause.)* So I guess sex is out of the question?

D: That's not funny.

C: I know.

                She watches him go.

In His Car

                *B and D are sitting together as in the front seat of
                the car.*

B: We sit in his car—for hours and hours. There's a lot
                of silence, a lot of staring. Out of the window, into
                his eyes. "I don't understand."

D: "I can't explain, it's just a feeling I have."

B: "Explain the feeling."

D: "I don't know. I've just lost my drive, my passion,
                my magic."

B: "Your magic?"

D: "I need to feel inspired again. I can't love my work
                and you too. It's draining me."

B: No. Tell me you don't love me anymore, that you
                don't find me attractive, that I'm nothing like the
                person you want to be with. Something I can grasp
                onto. Instead…

D: "But you're the most amazing person I know, this
                isn't about us, it's about me. I admire you so much,
                you're just so special…"

B: "I don't understand, I don't understand, I don't
                understand…" Panic. Confusion.

D: "There's nothing more I can say."

B: I can't say anything. Just, "Why?"

                (They kiss.) "Why?" *(They kiss.)* "Why?" *(They kiss.)*

And then his car door opens and he comes around to my door, opens it, takes my hand, leads me into my apartment to my bed, undresses me. "Take me, just take me please away anywhere take me."

D: "I love you."

B: And that is his final peace offering to me. He leaves before morning with a drawer full of stuff and my heart in his hand. I won't get out of bed for days.

A: Lights!

Director of the Breakup

A enters, hands B and D their scripts and sets them up in their positions. She gestures at B to start the scene.

A: Sound!

B: What will you do?

A: I ask him.

D: Quit my job, start listening, take that trip to India—

A: India?!?

D: ...work on my golf swing, maybe get the band back together. Find out what's missing. *(Embarrassed.)* This is really hard for me you know.

B: *(Apologetically.)* Sorry?

A: India? I thought we couldn't afford India? I thought you were too busy for us to go to India. Get the band back together? Who are you, the fucking Eagles? *(Snaps fingers at actors.)* Act!

B: *(Repeats.)* But I...

D: I'd rather we didn't rehash this.

B: Rehash this?

A: For months I have tried to talk, for months I have
          asked if anything's wrong, for months I have clung
          on for dear life to preserve this, to preserve us while
          he's withdrawn yet reassured me nothing's wrong.
          Months.

D: Let's not have a scene OK?

B: Uh, OK.

D: Let's do this as professionals.

A: Professional what? Professional breaker-uppers?

B: *(Nods.)* Sure.

D: Good. I've drawn up an alphabetized list of what's
          mine and what's yours, so maybe we should start
          from there.

          Silence. B is not reacting.

          I've covered all the bills for the month so you
          should be OK. *(Strokes B's hair. A pretends to stroke
          D's hair.)* This is, well this is hard for me you know.
          You've got to understand that.

A: I'm sorry, I should've made this easier on you by
          being the one who's so confused, who's fucked up
          over nothing, who has everything he's ever wanted
          and now doesn't know what to do with it. I'm sorry,
          I hadn't realized we'd assigned roles in the drama
          of you leaving me. I should've asked which role
          you'd prefer. I didn't say that of course. I just sat
          there. He said...

D: I'm going to be the bad guy in this. Nobody will
          understand. God, I'd much rather be the one who
          gets left than the one who leaves. I wish I could be
          the one staying...

A: How about wishing this wasn't happening, how about using that wish to get over your fucking self? You crybaby! You big fucking coward! I didn't say that either. *(To B.)* I muttered something about searching for your happiness…

B: Happiness…

A: And the strength…

B: Strength…

A: …it takes to find it.

B: What will I tell everyone?

A: Because I knew it would be me who'd be the spokesperson in all of this.

D: Tell them that I'm an idiot, that I'm making the biggest mistake of my life… You're so strong.

A: I stand there smiling my strong but vulnerable smile, watching him go.

A,B: Hey. It was nice living with you.

D: Yeah.

Reactions

C bursts onstage with a daytimer and pencil.

C: 7:30am: Time to get up!

8:00am: Making lunch for school bag, breakfast for the child, coffee for me.

8:30am: Take the child to school.

9:00am: Rush to the gym.

11am: Run out of the Y, leap into car and race to…

11:15: Meeting with the woman you need to get that contract from.

B: *(On phone in her pyjamas, eating popcorn, watching TV.)* Hi. I'm sorry I can't make it in—I think I have food poisoning or something. Yeah, oysters.

A: *(On hands and knees in full cleaning garb, scrubbing the floor.)* Yeah, I'm fine. It's for the best. No, honestly, I saw it coming, I was prepared. He needs his time. I'm OK. There's just so much to get done. I'm so busy, feeding the homeless, reading to the blind, working out, eating well.

C: *(Continues with her list of things to do as A and B speak—she finishes this section as A says "I'm so busy." above, then takes a breath and continues softly under A and B's lines unti "11 pm", which stands alone.)*

12 noon: Drive back to the school—it's volunteer-in-the-library day!

2pm: Home! Check messages, get dinner ready for the child and the sitter.

3pm: Dress for work, rush out the door with a peanut butter bagel in hand.

3:30pm: Work till 9pm. Done.

B: Hi. I'd like to order a large pizza. Extra cheese with mushrooms, pineapple, pepperoni and green olives.

A: I'm reading a lot about relationships, you know, so if he ever needs to talk… I'm doing a lot of work on me…

B: Hi. I just ordered a pizza. I'm sorry I'm going to have to cancel that order.

C: *(Still under A and B's lines.)* 9:30pm: Home, pay off sitter, call her a cab.

10pm: Pick up house, do dinner dishes, check on the girl.

10:30pm: Answer phone messages, do paperwork for tomorrow, check schedule, set up the child's knapsack for school, check her homework, set table for breakfast.

Lines no longer overlap.

11pm: Tuck the blue sweater you made him into the fireplace, pour a little lighter fluid on it and set a match to it.

A: It's not like it was a surprise or anything. Oh yeah, I'm as much to blame as he is.

C: 11:45pm: Pour a stiff Scotch.

B: Hi. I'd like to order the "One Hundred Classic Love Songs" double disc.

C: 12 midnight: Shower, cry.

12:30am: Soap has melted in your hand. Knock on the bathroom door, "Mummy, I need a drink of water."

12:35am: Tuck her in, dripping wet, with towel falling off.

12:45am: Collapse on own bed.

B: Hi. I'm a Sagittarius. Are there any new planetary developments?

C: 7:30am: Wake up, stiff. Wet hair has dried in tangles. Drool crusted in corners of mouth.

A: He wants to be friends.

C: "Mummy, why are you sleeping in a towel? What's for breakfast?"

Bridesmaids

> *As a hopeful 50s girl group song plays, A, B and C perform a choreographed routine of putting on their lipstick, makeup, doing the hair and finally, putting on the happy face they will take to their first public appearance. The music ends as the girls are asked:*

A,B,C: Hey you, where's the boy?

> *And they reply.*

C: Oh, he's not,

A: Well…

B: We're not…

A,B: What?

A,B,C: Together.

A,C: Wow, you look great considering…

B: Oh, I'm fine. He'll be back.

A,B: I can't believe it.

C: He left…he left…

A,B: Oooooh babe.

C,B: How are you? I heard, I'm soooooooooo sorry. You guys were so perfect together.

A: You think so?

A,C: So, what's his deal?

B: He just needs to work some stuff out.

B,C: I mean I thought you guys were, like, it, you know?

A: Well, you know.

B,C: He-has-no-idea-what-he's-losing. NOW-tell-me-
            everything.

A: Maybe if we'd gone on vacation.

B: Maybe if I'd let him alphabetize my CDs.

C: Maybe if I'd worn more makeup.

A,B: Look at you!

C: Yeah.

A,B: Yeah, so are you, you know, are you?

C: What?

A,B: Pregnant!

C: No, not pregnant, no.

A,B: Well, I didn't mean…

C: Maybe if I'd had skinnier legs.

B: Maybe if I'd tried to understand football.

A: Maybe if I'd stayed up late.

B,C: You guys were so great, what a couple! How tragic
            for you, what are you now, thirty?

A: Twenty-nine.

B,C: Ugh. I mean, if you two couldn't make it work, who
            can?

C: He lee-ee-eeft…he leeeeeft…

A,B: Oh my God.

A: Look, it's going to be OK.

B: He's just got a lot of stuff going on.

A: Maybe if I'd worn plum eye shadow instead of
            beige.

B:	Maybe if I'd said I didn't want children.
C:	Maybe if I'd watched more hockey.
A,B:	So what are you going to do?
B:	He just needs some more time.
A:	Maybe if I'd had better underwear.
B:	Maybe if I'd walked on the north side of the street.
C:	Maybe if I'd worked out more.
B,C:	Well I am devastated, just devastated. This throws my dream of happily-ever-after right out the window.
A:	I'm sorry, we tried, we really did. I know we let you down, I'm sorry. I know.
B,C:	Just remember, everything happens for a reason.
A:	Maybe if I'd let him read at the table.
B:	Maybe if I hadn't talked to my mother so much.
C:	Maybe if I'd let him pick the movies.
A,B:	Say it.
C:	What?
A,B:	Say, he left me.
C:	*(Little voice.)* He left me.
A,B:	Again.
C:	He left me.
A,B:	Again.
C:	He left me.

A,B:	Again!
C:	*(Shrieks.)* He left me!
A,B:	There now, doesn't that feel good?
A:	Maybe if I'd just been better.
B:	Maybe if my face was oval.
C:	Maybe if I'd let him become a Mountie.

The Mountie

D enters enthusiastically.

D:	I want to join the RCMP!
C:	What?
D:	I want to join the RCMP.
C:	You want to be a Mountie? You want to be a cop?
D:	Yes.
C:	But…
D:	But what?
C:	You hate guns. You can't shoot guns. You hate guns.
D:	You never support me. I can never count, y'know, on you, for support.
C:	But…
D:	Because you won't support me. I come to you, y'know, just needing a little, a little, all I want from you is…
C:	But you can't shoot a gun.
D:	…support—not all policemen shoot guns.

C: Yes they do. Policemen have guns.

D: I could sit behind a desk. I could solve crimes. Do desk work. Answer phones. Help people.

C: You'd have to do basic training! You'd have to train! They'd have to send you to police school and you'd have to shoot a gun! You hate guns! You're a gun-hating pacifist professor!

D: You think I couldn't do it, don't you? You think I couldn't...do you think I'm not capable—is that what you think?

C: No, I—yes. Yes! I think you couldn't. You couldn't because you don't want to. You're not a gun-shooter you're—where did this come from?

D: It came from me, from what I want, from you not supporting me, supporting me in my choices, in my—what do you think of me, anyway? Do you think I just dreamed this up? I just woke up this morning and thought, "Hey, maybe I'll be a Mountie?" *(He pulls out a cigarette.)*

C: No, I, I don't—you're a thirty-five-year-old *(He lights the cigarette and coughs.)* asthmatic professor who hates guns—it's an assumption I've—I don't know—no—look, honey, I do want to support you if that's what you want, I'll help you, we'll do this, I'll support you through basic training or whatever it is they do.

D: You've never believed in me, have you? Never trusted me, never—God. Never mind. God!

         He leaves in disgust, coughing.

Divine Secrets

D: Did you get the movie?

B: I didn't get *Contempt*.

D: What did you get?

B: *Divine Secrets of the Ya-Ya Sisterhood.* I think you'll
            really like it.

D: But *Contempt* is Godard's finest hour. It's the
            epitome of French New Wave.

B: But it's got subtitles. Besides, I got the Ya-Ya girls.
            It's Sandra Bullock and Ashley Judd.

D: *(Sigh.)* Have you seen my other black sock?

B: Oh, it's probably with the rest of your laundry. It's
            clean.

D: You did my laundry?

B: Yeah, you're always leaving your clothes here, so I
            threw them in with some of mine.

D: I'd rather you didn't do my laundry.

B: It's no problem.

D: I don't live here.

B: You might as well.

D: Did you pick up some beer?

So...

            A and D are offstage at different sides of the stage —
            for the first few lines their heads poke in and out, just
            missing each other.

A: So... How was your day?

D: Busy.

A: Hi.

D: Hi.

A: Is anything wrong?

D: I got the dry-cleaning.

> *He shows her and continues on with his busy busy routine.*

A: I miss you.

D: Traffic was crazy.

A: I miss you.

D: Idiot drivers.

A: I feel like I could poke my finger right through you.

D: The 401 was a parking lot.

A: You're going away a little bit at a time.

D: Turned out a truck rolled.

A: I'm forgetting what your skin tastes like.

D: I should've taken the QEW.

> *He settles down half offstage on a chair — there but not.*

A: I read when one of your senses goes, the others overcompensate for the loss, so why are mine going numb?

D: I've got some paperwork to do.

A: I thought you were the one. I even said it out loud for everyone to hear, "This is the one." We bought dishes together. We signed Christmas cards with both our names on them. Merry Christmas, I love you, I love you too, Happy Birthday, Happy

Anniversary, Happily ever after, love me and The Coward.

Messages

B is onstage alone with her cellphone, trying to change her answering machine message.

B: Hello, no one's here to take your call right now. No one's here.

Hello, unfortunately I am unable to come to the phone at the moment because he—shit!

Hi, I'm sorry I'm not here to take your call. If you're looking for "Magic Man," HE is no longer practically living here, using up all my hot water, eating my groceries. If you'd like to contact him, he can be reached at 1-800-I-Need-Some-Fucking-Inspiration!

Ken and Barbie

A bunch of toys fly in from the wings and C wearily comes onstage picking them up and cleaning up. She picks up Barbie and settles down centre and talks through the doll.

C: Hello, my name's Barbie. What's yours? I have an amazing apartment, a fabulous figure, a great career and a sensational single life!

(Now speaking as Ken as he pops up.) Hi, Barbie, I'm Ken. Wanna get married?

(Barbie.) OK! *(Barbie and Ken make with the kissy face, mwuh mwuh mwuh.)*

(Ken.) Love you!

(Barbie.) Love you too!

(Ken.) No ,love you more!

(Barbie.) I love you so much I'm going to work you through grad school.

(Ken.) OK!

(Barbie.) La la la la la la la—work, work, work, work—

(Ken.) Study, study, study, study.

(Barbie.) Work!

(Ken.) Study! *(Barbie.)* Work! *(Ken.)* Study!

(Barbie.) Work work work!

(Ken.) Barbie, I'm home—and guess what? I got a big fat tenure position today!

(Barbie.) Oh goodie, Ken! Now you're making money, we can pay off your student loan, buy that new car, I can resume my career...

(Ken.) Barbie, I want to be a Mountie.

(Barbie.) What?

(Ken.) A Mountie, Barbie, a Mountie.

(Barbie.) But Ken—

(Ken.) You don't support me, Barbie—I don't love you and I never did.

(Barbie.) Yes you did. You did. We had the motorcycle, and the Barbie camper and the kissy kissy.

(Ken.) Nope, never loved you. Want to be a Mountie.

(Barbie.) But what about Barbie Baby Kelly? *(C pulls out a much larger doll and makes her cry.)* Waah, waah!

(Ken.) Leave Kelly out of this, Barbie! *(C chucks Kelly over her shoulder.)* I love her, it's you I can't live with.

(Barbie.) But Ken… *(Kelly.)* waah waah!

(Ken.) Sorry Barbie, but a man's gotta do what a man's gotta do. *(C makes Ken walk away and get on the Barbie motorcycle.)*

(Making the appropriate noises.) Vroom vroom! Waah waah!

(In C's real voice, to Barbie.) Listen Barbie, are you just going to take this lying down!?!

(Barbie.) No! This I give you Ken and that I give you Ken and take that and that and take that and…

> *Barbie beats up Ken and C, as a final coup de grace, bites his head off. A appears and clears her throat.*

C: Sorry.

> *C exits guiltily.*

Box Poetry

> *A is writing, then gets up on top of her box of cleaning things and reads what she's been working on.*

A: Things you should know. THINGS YOU SHOULD KNOW!

I'm just fine.

Everyone says I look fabulous.

Groceries are cheaper without you.

My father never liked you.

Your sister's a bitch.

If you quit the firm, how will you get rich?

How's the band, the band, the band the band the band— "Here they come, the boys in the bright white sports car" —it's over!

I lied, you really can see your bald spot.

Fortune 500— Hm, don't see your name on the list.

India, India, why was I so in-to-ya?

It's not like I thought we'd last.

I barely even miss you.

She picks up her box and goes.

Spleenectomy

B and C are working out on elliptical trainers: they each have two sticks in their hands they are pumping back and forth. B is wearing headphones and clearly doesn't want to listen.

C: Oh, did I tell you? I'm having a spleenectomy.

B: What?

C: *(Shouting at her; B gives up and takes off her headphones.)* A spleenectomy. I think I'm developing a thing on my spleen right now.

B: When did this happen?

C: It happened two days ago, when Mountie Boy invited me to his big party. I'm telling him I can't come because it's the day I've been scheduled for the spleenoplasty.

B: Are you insane? What happens if he asks you about how it went?

C: Oh he will, even he can't be so completely unfeeling.
        He asks and I tell him…tell him that they took some
        more x-rays and now they're not sure.

B: You know what? I don't think it works that way.

C: What the hell do you know about spleens? What
        do you know about spleencoscopies? I could have
        my spleen removed and be walking around today.
        That's it. I tell him I did have it removed. "Oh, poor
        me, I've got no spleen."

B: What the hell does a spleen do anyway?

C: I don't know. I could read up on it. Read up on my
        spleen. I should have this all figured out before I
        have to RSVP.

B: You are certifiably insane. You have really and truly
        lost it.

C: No, no, this could be really great. He calls me up,
        all contrite, to ask me how I am and I tell him I'm
        fine, a little weak… He might offer to go with me
        to the hospital. No, I want to go with my friends,
        my true friends, my woman friends, my support
        through this terrible, terrible time. And when I do
        see him again I'll be wrapped in blankets, looking
        pale and wan—thank God for makeup, eh?—and
        I'll have trouble getting up to greet him… I have to
        remember to do this in the daytime while the kid's
        at school and can't blow my cover—oh this could
        really guilt him out but good. Oh it is so, what's that
        movie you like? With the Empire State Building?

B: Yeah, but didn't Cary Grant really love her? Wasn't
        he being noble?

C: Yeah, noble schnoble. I want him to feel bad, really
        bad, nasty bad. (Pumping away demonically as the
        scene ends.)

Garlic Press

> *D enters gingerly.*

D: Hello?

A: Hi! *(A crashing sound from offstage.)* Fuck!

D: Are you OK?

> *A enters from stage right.*

A: What do you mean?

D: Well, you sounded a little weird on the phone.

A: Oh no I'm fine. I couldn't sleep so I re-grouted the bathroom tile, then I ended up tackling the closet in the hall and some of the kitchen drawers and I found some things of yours and I just thought you might need them, what with you setting up house and everything, and oh yeah, I was cleaning the medicine cabinet when it hit me! It's January! And I thought ah! It's January and I know your allergies are crazy this time of year and I know what you're like not taking your medication, so I thought you could take some of this new stuff I'm using of course my allergies bug me in August but God allergies are allergies aren't they? You seem wheezy are you wheezy?

D: I'm fine! The place looks great. You've been busy.

A: Yeah. Busy busy.

D: Sorry about this, forgetting this stuff…

A: Mustn't have been on your list..

D: I thought I took everything.

A: Well you must've forgot.

D: Yeah, must've what with everything.

A: Yeah, with everything. So, you're good?

D: Mmmm, yeah, great, I was at Derek and Wendy's wedding over the weekend.

A: Really? Wow, how long have they been together?

D: Just a year. I guess they just knew.

A: Hmmm, imagine that. Oh, you know what? You forgot the garlic press.

D: Right. No, no you take it.

A: No, I couldn't, you use that garlic press.

D: I know but so do you. You always use it to cook, my God you love garlic. You are eating aren't you? You look thin.

A: No, yeah, I'm fine, I'm eating, it's just, I mean I can buy a new garlic press.

D: But why buy one when it's already—

        He freezes and the lights change as A loses it and says what she really wants to say.

A: Take your goddamn garlic press you piece of shit coward. And all your cookbooks for the meals you never made, while you're at it, take the wine rack, drink yourself silly and choke on your own vomit!

        The lights change back and it's sweetness and light again.

D: —when it's already there.

A: No really, you take it. I'll pick up a new one.

D: Are you sure?

A: I'm sure.

D: You take care of you, OK?

A: 'Kay.

D: I should… uh, I've got band practice.

A: See you.

D: Not if I see you first.

Hail Mary

B comes onstage and kneels, curlers in her hair and fuzzy dressing gown on.

If I will love back into my life, no, if I keep forward in my life, my life will move forward with me, no, if I burn everything that has to do with him…no!

Hail Mary, full of grace, blessed are you among women. But do you know much about men? Pray for me, now, at the hour of my heart's death. I swear, I will sacrifice all my earthly burdens. I already have three garbage bags ready for the Goodwill. I've been meaning to teach Sunday School classes, but I haven't been able to get out of bed just yet. Mary, the Bible says even if you have the faith to move mountains but do not have love, you are nothing. Can we cut a deal? I promise that I won't stop praying if he comes back. I know, I know, in Grade Nine you helped Jimmy and I get back together and then I dumped him and stopped praying. But it's different this time. This time I love him, Mary. Can't you see that? Jesus. Oh, no. God, I'm sorry. Please make him come back. Please, make him love me again.

My Relationship vs. Your Relationship

Doorbell rings and B frantically gets ready, ditching dressing gown, curlers and tidying up, setting up table and two chairs, then opens door.

D: Hi. Sorry I'm late.

B: It's OK. I'm glad you called. It's good to see you. You must be busy.

D: Yeah, I am. Look, I'm sorry to bother you.

B: No, not at all.

D: I can't stay or anything.

B: …Of course, no, and I have a lot to do…

D: Thanks for coming… I just came to give you your keys back.

B: Oh…right, my keys.

D: Yeah. So, here they are.

B: Yep, there they are.

She just stares at them and doesn't move to take them.

D: I forgot to give you them the other night.

B: Yeah, the other night.

She takes the keys.

D: Well, I'll talk to you.

B: Thanks. For bringing the keys.

D: No problem. It's the least I could do.

B: You know, I still don't understand.

D: Look, I've tried to explain.

B: But it was the fairytale relationship.

D: The Frog Prince.

B: Cinderella—you just got chicken. *(No response.)* It was like poetry.

D: It was a made-for-TV movie.

B: *An Affair to Remember.*

D: *When Worlds Collide.*

B: But, we never fought.

D: Exactly! That's not normal. *(He sits at the table.)*

B: But you were so happy. *(She sits too, opposite him.)*

D: I know.

B: And we were so good together and so comfortable.

D: That's it. Comfortable. But, I stopped writing late at night.

B: Because you said you wrote better in the morning.

D: Only because when you were up doing your *Buns of Steel*, I had peace and quiet.

B: But that was our ritual though.

D: Your ritual.

B: OK, then. You started the rituals.

D: Name one.

B: Tuesday night—Sandwich Night. Whoever's is better doesn't have to clean up.

D: To make up for Boys' Night the night before.

B: What about Quiet Night then, Date Night?

D: I lost my magic!

B: That's not good enough. *(She puts her hand out to him.)*

D: Fine. You wanna know? You really wanna know?

I hate *(He grabs her hand and suddenly they are arm-wrestling.)* the smell of Downy.

B: It was to drown out your smelly socks.

D: You're a sloppy tea pourer!

B: At least I don't leave the teabags in the sink.

D: I love coffee!

B: Well, you should have told me!

D: I hate your disposable razors!

B: I hate your liquid soap.

D: Well, Dove sucks.

B: Toilet paper has to be put in roll down, not roll up!

      She's starting to get the upper hand.

D: Unbearable.

B: I stole one black sock from your laundry every week just to drive you mad!

D: But...

B: I secretly plotted to destroy all of your friendships—because that's who I really am. I watched you type in your password so I could check your messages while you were in the shower.

D: ...you...

B: And all this time you were thinking that it was just the little things that were getting to you, you couldn't even see the major plot to take over your life!

      She slams his hand down triumphantly. He crawls off as A and C enter. They all watch him with pity.

*C is carrying a tray full of shots of tequila, lemon
wedges and three salt shakers.*

Mythology

B: I think he still loves me.

C: How?

B: By the way he looks at me, the things he, if things
weren't so, well just stuff.

C: Really? What stuff? What looks? Name one.

A: Easy, I think she's just saying that she—

C: No! She can't think like that. She has to get on with
it, she has to realize—

A: What she needs to do is—

B: Hey! She's in the room! Look, maybe he loves me,
maybe he, anyway, if I want to believe in us, I will.
It's my fairytale.

C: *(Mocking.)* It's my fairytale…

B: Hey!

A: Sometimes I think our fairytale was too much to
live up to.

C: What do you mean?

A: Our story, our tale. Everyone thought we were so
perfect, the mythology of us was so fabulous even
we couldn't live up to it.

B: But it's not like it wasn't true, remember the sonnets
he wrote you, the breakfasts in bed, that time in
France, carrying you through that field of—

A: Yeah, yeah, yeah, but at some point did he do it just
to keep up with expectations? I did. I didn't want

to wait for him at the subway every night, but it became one of those things that made us "us." Everyone else loved the romance of it, but stand outside the subway station when it's 30 below and see how romantic you feel. Maybe he was suffocating in our mythology.

C: Here's a myth—happily ever after! Next time no mythology for me. Write your letters, send me your flowers, piggyback me across the damn desert but not until you've figured out what you want to be when you grow up. Lick drink suck.

They all do.

B: Maybe mythology isn't a bad thing, maybe it binds you. He knows me like no one else. I'll never have that again.

C: Yes you will and the next time it will be better, and the time after that it will be better than the time before and after that—

B: No it won't.

C: Yes it will! Sweetie it's hard, but it's over, now there's a whole world of great stories out there, new myths waiting to happen. Lick drink suck.

And again, they do.

Is That Helping?

The lights change and D is suddenly a drunk anonymous guy sitting at the back of the house.

D: Hey you, is that helping?

C: What?

D: You know what I'm talking about.

B: What?

D: You. You know I'm talking to you.

A: What?

D: You heard me.

B: But I...

D: No buts, honey—do you think he's going to come back?

A: Well, I don...

D: In your dreams. Do you think he's even thinking about you any more?

C: Well, I...

D: Get a life.

A,B,C: I have a life.

D: And that's what we are talking about here. Get a life. Get over it. It's over. Do you hear me? Over. Your friends are sick to death of hearing about it. Hearing about you, whining on and on and on...

B: No,

A: not my friends,

C: my friends love me.

D: Oh get a grip! You know how your friend Jen is never home any more—she's "really busy" at work?

A: Yes, she's got

C: that big project

B: coming up and...

D: Bullshit! She just can't stand to listen to you any more! She got call waiting specially for you! She's screening her calls because you are driving her crazy.

C: No,

B: not Jen—

A: not my Jen…

D: How much of this do you think any human being can stand? Three-hour monologues about how much you miss him…

A,B,C: But I love him…

D: You love him? You love him? Wow, and he must really love you too—I guess that's why he dumped you and cleaned out his side of the drawer.

B: He just needs some…

D: How little self-esteem do you have, anyway? Didn't your parents love you?

A: My parents love me…

D: Yeah well clearly not enough. Were you breast fed?

C: I don't…

D: You have got some serious issues you're going to have to tackle here, honey. Get on it while you've still got enough going on to find someone new. Time's a-wasting. You're not gettin' any younger. Hey, is that a grey hair?

A,B,C: Wha???

Meanwhile…

The lights change and the girls are having another shot and trying to regroup.

Honour

C: Hey hey hey, just 'cause he left you before you got it together to leave him—

A: I had plenty of chances to leave. Plenty. Opportunities. Chances.

B: I know.

A: But I didn't.

B: No.

A: Y'know that? I didn't.

B: No, you didn't.

A: And y'know why? Y'wanna know why?

C: Why?

A: Because I'm honourable. I honoured what we had.

B: You are.

A: I am. I am. I honour…things. Sacred things. Love. And honour. I honoured…honour. Y'know?

B: I know.

A: But he, he—

B: Well, he doesn't know what honour is.

C: Clearly.

A: He doesn't. He never did.

C: Let's key his car.

A: I loved that car. I honoured that car.

C: I miss Mountie Boy's car.

A: You honoured the Mountie's car.

B: Mountie Boy had a car you could honour. I don't miss Magic Man's car at all.

C: We had a better marriage when we were poor, but…

B: It was a K-car!

C: …I looked so good in that car. I fit in that car.

B: You did fit with his car…

C: And his parents—geez, I loved his parents.

A: Honour your parents. Honour the Mountie's parents.

C: Let's go key The Coward's car.

A: I don't honour The Coward's car. I honour The Coward's parents. He doesn't honour his parents. I did. I do. I honour them.

C: That's a lot of honour.

A: A lot of honour.

C: Where does he live now?

A: Who?

C: The Coward.

A: The Coward?

C: Does he park on the street?

A: No, in the lane—there's a lane. I don't think there's a garage. If there was, he'd be rehearsing with the band in there. (*Takes another swig.*)

B: He doesn't honour his car.

C: I'd honour that car. I love that car. Not as much as Mountie Boy's car, but I'd look pretty good in Coward's car too.

A: *(Galvanized, suddenly.)* Let's go.

B: What?

A: He doesn't honour his car, neither should we.

C: Yea, baby.

B: What? What do you mean?

A: *(Brandishing keys.)* Call us a cab, baby doll. We're movin' out.

B: I'll be right there.

            A and C leave the stage, leaving B alone for a moment.

About Last Night

B: I've watched *An Affair to Remember* twenty-seven times. Last week I saw this movie with Rob Lowe and Demi Moore called *About Last Night* and I cried and cried when they divided their stuff. But then he figured it all out and came back. And then I read the play, the real play of the movie—it's called *Sexual Perversity in Chicago* and you know they don't even end up together again in the real play. I mean why would they, it's called *Sexual Perversity in Chicago* for God's sake. So then I think if they don't end up together in the play, why did they make them end up together in the movie? The play came first so why don't you leave the ending the way it is and not change it to pretty it all up and make it seem all happy and perfect. Of course I saw the movie before I read the play so now what am I supposed to think, that's it's not really a happy ending? Maybe nothing is. Maybe I did have the love story of my life and I'll never have it again. Just like the play, it ends and that's that.

Mummy

> *As B leaves she becomes the voice of C's child momentarily; C is entering and hears her say.*

B: Mummy, why did you let Daddy leave?

> *B exits and leaves C speaking out to the audience to her child.*

C: Well, you see, Daddy and I spent a long time talking about this, and Daddy was very unhappy. Not with you, just very unhappy about a lot of things that he couldn't figure out. And he thought that maybe if he went somewhere and lived on his own for a while, that maybe he might be happier.

And after a while he realized that it was a little easier for him to live on his own—it made him feel better than he had before. So, he and I decided that it would be better for you to live with me in our old house and that way you would get to see a happier Daddy sometimes instead of an unhappy Daddy all the time.

You know what? More than anything else in the whole wide world, Daddy loves you. He loves you more than this. *(She holds her arms out wide.)*

And the hardest thing that Daddy has ever done in his life was leaving our house where we all lived together. Because there is nothing in Daddy's life that he likes better than waking up in the room down the hall from you.

You know what? When Daddy first told me that he couldn't live here any more, I got mad, because I wanted him to stay living with us.

It's a crummy thing for grown-ups to do to kids, change their world around. But it doesn't mean you don't have a Daddy, and it doesn't mean that your Daddy loves you any less, it just means you don't get quite as much of him as you used to. But that's OK—you can get mad at us about that. You're allowed. It's OK.

Keying the Car

> *B and C enter with flashlights, hand one to C and all three plunge into the audience to find The Coward's car.*

B: I don't like this. I don't like this at all.

A: It's over here.

C: I love this neighbourhood. Look at all these backyards. Even the garages are nice.

B: This is not right. This is just not right.

A: We haven't done anything yet. We're just walking in the lane here.

B: At midnight. In the dark. With flashlights. Behind your ex's house.

C: So?

B: Look, I have serious is-sues about all this.

A: What?

B: I have is-sues.

A: Ishues?

B: Yes, is-sues.

C: Ishues.

A: Yeah.

C: Say it.

B: Is-sues.

A: Ish-ues.

B: (Repeating.) Is-sues.

C: Say Ish.

B: Ish.

A: Yews.

B: Yews.

C: Ish. Yews.

B: Ish. Yews.

A: Ishues.

B: Is-sues.

C: Fuck!

A: Ohmygod.

C: What?

A: It's Coward.

B: Turn off your flashlight.

A: I always told him to pull the curtains—I always said people could see in—he said, "What people?"

B: Don't look—don't look! We're not peeping toms here…we haven't sunk that far…

C: Yeah, yeah I came here to key his car, but I'm not going to spy on him?

B: Don't you find that a little…

C: What, unethical?

B: Criminal.

A: What he did to me was criminal.

C: Shit.

B: What.

A: Who's that? *(She drops to the ground. B crouches behind the car, C turns flashlight on again, stands up, then loudly…)*

C: Who is that?

A: I don't believe it. It's the Office Bitch.

B: Didn't he leave you because he wanted to be alone?

A: She's sitting on my end of the couch. That's my spot. She's sitting in my place.

C: So is he, really.

B: You let him have that couch?

A: She's going to sleep with him. Why would she want to sleep with him?

C: You wanted to sleep with him.

A: He said he wanted to be alone. Alone. Not alone with other women. He said.

B: Look, he's just falling into a rebound relationship. They never last. You are doing everything right, mourning the relationship, dealing with it. You can't learn to be in a relationship until you learn to be alone.

C: Yeah, but while she's out getting big and strong and learning to be alone, he is clearly getting laid.

B: Shhh! Look, he was bound to start dating sooner or later. Geez, he's looking over here—he hears us—guys let's get out of here.

C: *(Shining flashlight in her own face.)* Hey! Asshole! That's her end of the couch.

B: Stop that. Get down.

A: *(In a heap on the ground.)* My couch. My spot. Honour my couch!

C: Yeah, you asshole—I've got keys here, how much do you like the finish on your cute little Beemer?

B: Stop that. *(To house.)* Sorry! I'm really sorry! Go back to what you were doing!

A: No!!

C: DON'T MAKE ME USE THESE!

MALE VOICE: *(Offstage from the other side of the stage than where they are looking.)* Hey! What's going on out there?

B: Geez. *(To voice, stage left.)* Sorry! Sorry! Just leaving!

MALE VOICE: *(O.S.)* People are trying to sleep here.

C: People are trying to do a bit more than sleep here—people are talking about JUSTICE here! What is RIGHT. What is HONOURABLE. Do you hear me?

MALE VOICE: *(O.S.)* I'm calling the police now.

B: No! No! No police—we're going! I'm sorry. Get up *(To A.)* GET UP.

A: My boyfriend. My Coward. My couch spot. *(Weeping incoherently.)*

B: *(Turning to C.)* Don't you go near that car. Give me those. *(Grabs keys.)* Get hold of yourselves. Both of you. You are crazy. Both of you. Do you know that? Crazy. *(To voice.)* Y'know what? Call the police, mister. Go ahead. Tell them to bring straitjackets. I am out of here. I am out of patience. You guys are nuts. Call me—when you are ready to be reasonable human beings and DEAL with this.

Alright? Reasonable. Human. Beings. Good night. *(She leaves.)*

Long pause.

C: Geez. What got into her? *(She runs off after her, leaving A alone with her flashlight and a box of stuff which she pulls out one by one to illustrate her points throughout her rant.)*

The Rant

A: I have been dating for 16 years. In that time I have had no offers of marriage. In 16 years, I have lived with two men. Told at least six that I loved them, and meant it at the time. And I'm sure someone said they loved me back. None of them became like major rock stars, a few are balding, one is a supermodel in Milan. So is his wife. She is younger than me, they have a child. My friend sent me his marriage announcement from the *Gravenhurst Times*. Underneath it she wrote: "It was almost you babe!" For the record, I broke up with him. I have slept with twenty people, it's not a lot, it's barely one a year. Not all were Irish, some weren't even nice. All, at the time, were attractive. I've never slept with an accountant or a businessman, which may explain the state of my finances. I've slept with too many musicians and not enough doctors, but the musicians were the ones who were around. Once I dated a cop and a criminal at the same time—but they weren't on the same case or anything so it's not like it was illegal. I don't just random date and dump. I don't usually sleep with other people's boyfriends. I inspire people you know. I have had three songs written about me and a piece of Japanese performance art. One of the songs got a lot of play on Much Music and Much More Music. Naomi Campbell played me in the video; I would've preferred Helen Hunt, but

Naomi is really coming into her own as an actress. I am never envious when friends are happy with the little things like weddings and babies, I know my time will come. People keep telling me that I'm in my prime, that it'll happen when I least expect it. My phone gets cut off when I least expect it, I get a yeast infection when I least expect it, I get dumped, break out, laid off when I least expect it. When it comes to meeting Mr. Right, we always expect it. It's the unwritten thing to do in everyone's dayplanner—go for groceries, fix the sink, make the bed, meet Mr. Right. And then when he or she arrives, we substitute "meet" for "hold on to," "do not let go of"… I didn't hold on too tight, he let go of. I do not deserve this!

Maybe I Should

C and B march out and join A.

A: Maybe we should…

C: Talk. She got a great report card. Maybe I should…

B: Call him. My stars are really aligned. Maybe we should…

A: Get together for…

C: A drink. *(They all whip out phones.)*

A,B,C: Hi. It's Me. What's your next Thursday like?

Reunion Sex

Lights up to reveal A and D having primitive animal sex, her straddling the man in one crazy contorted pose behind and above a hanging bedsheet.

D: What are you doing?

A: What do you mean?

D: This, you, this—

A: I'm riding you, screwing you, choking your chain—

D: You're what?

A: I'm straddling you. I'm banging you. We're making the two-backed beast. What's wrong? Why are you being like this? Just relax...

D: Why am I? No, this is not like you...

        He moves as if to get away from her—she doesn't let him go and continues to ride him.

A: Yes it is, yes it is, it is, this is it baby, this is me, in touch and on top, oh yeah, you're not gonna get this anyplace else, do you like it like this, does the Office Bitch do it like this, does baby like it when I ride the big purple python...

        They disappear down below the sheet and then suddenly D appears again, this time with C wrapped around him.

C: Oh baby—Oh baby! Oh YES! (*She leans into him, then pulls from between them a suitcase.*)

D: What—what is—what the hell is that?

C: Your mother—my relationship with your mother. She calls you her baby doll and had an asthma attack when she walked into my apartment.

D: I—

        Fumbles towards her, arms around the suitcase, hands going "Come in Tokyo."

C: (*Pulls out another one.*) Drinking—here's the drinking. Remember when you got trashed at my uncle's Christmas party?

D: Uh…

C: I love you honey I love you. *(Another one.)*

Oh no—your flirtation with Alex the lawyer. Or did you ever

(Another one.) sleep with her?

> *D is waving arms desperately trying to be sexy—around all the suitcases.*

C: AAAaaaah!!!! Smoking! *(Another one.)* Cats!

(Another.) My brother! *(Another.)* The office party!

(Another.) Body hair! *(Another.)* Oral sex! *(A huge one.)*

D: *(Practically buried, muffled.)* mmeye—mmmm want—mmmyou—mmyou…

> *We hear B and D building to a climax behind the sheet and then they pop up together, post-coital.*

B: Whoa! Oh God, oh God, oh God OH MY GOD! How come it was never like that before?

D: I don't know.

B: Maybe it was because we were too inhibited.

D: Maybe.

B: By the pressures of it all.

D: Yeah, but…

B: And now we can just be free of all that.

D: Free?

B: God it feels good! We can just be…

D: What?

B: Together.

            Blackout.

Answering Machine

            Answering machine beeps.

D: *(V.O.)* Hi, uh, it's me, uh… How are you? Uh, um,
            listen, about last night…I think it's so great that
            you're getting past this, past us, and moving on and
            I don't want you to get the wrong idea, I don't want
            to mess up your process—I don't want to be unfair
            to you—that's the last thing I would want to do to
            you. So, like, you take care of yourself and we'll
            see you around somewhere. Sometime. Alright?
            Alright. I'm sure you feel the same way. Let's not
            make the same mistake twice, eh? *(Awkward laugh.)*
            Yeah. Bye now. It was—good to see you. Bye.

            *The lights have come up slowly throughout the
            answering machine message to find all three girls
            caught, horrified, centre stage, listening.*

Breakups Anonymous

            *The girls take a deep breath and begin their cleansing
            ritual with a rainstick.*

A,B,C: Sister Goddess, Mother Moon, show me that I will
            heal soon.

            *Before each person talks, she turns the phallic
            rainstick over and holds it in front of her against
            her chest.*

A: Love songs tell us that the nights are the hardest to
            get through, but nights are the easiest. At night you
            can lie in the dark and cry. At night you are alone

with your thoughts and there's no pretense of being
capable, of doing a job, of being in a conversation, of
being present. I decide to emerge from my cocoon
and enter the world again. I am about to make my
first appearance as a solo artist. I arrive and I am
so alone. I am alone in a room full of people. But
I will be OK. I tell stories that make people laugh,
I talk about how busy we are at work, busy, busy,
no time for myself, I barely had time to slip into
this fabulous dress, I toss my hair, another funny
story, smile, somebody else says something and
everybody laughs. I am dying here. I want to look
across the room and meet his eyes and know we're
thinking the same thing. I want to be in the middle
of a conversation and feel his hand on my back. I
want to talk in "we"s again. I want to read him stuff
from the newspaper that I know will make him
laugh, I want to flirt while we do dishes, I want to
talk in "we"s again. Will we ever be us again?

*The other women thank her and exchange supportive
looks.*

C: He left me. He left me. Every time I say it it gets a
little easier. Every time I say it I cry a little less. I
have nine years of happy memories and six months
of awful ones. I am no longer permitted to share the
happy ones. My wedding dress lives in a cardboard
coffin from the drycleaners underneath the spare
bed in my parents' house. Will my daughter want
to wear it? Or is it tainted? Marriage took me by
surprise. I never even wanted to get married. He
wanted it, wanted it desperately. He wanted the
wife, the house, the kid, the whole nine yards. Then
he changed his mind and oops! he's single and I've
got...the house and the kid and the whole nine
yards. How did I get here?

The other women clap lightly and supportively.

B: When it comes down to it, it's not that I was too

strong for him, that I was too creative, that I was too healthy, that I was too perfect, it's that I always spilled my tea when I poured it, that I put the toilet paper in the holder roll down instead of roll up, that I always put chapstick on before I went to bed even if he was going to kiss it off. These are all the things he fell in love with in the first place, but at some point he chose not to. Love is a choice and he chose not to.

It's not about the leaving—that's not it. It's not even about him anymore. What it is about is that part of me that I can't find anymore, that precious kernel of myself he took when he walked out that day. That he carries it around with him and doesn't even know he has it—that is what this is about. I've retraced our entire four years together and now I have this map in front of me of where we ended up, I still can't figure out how we got here. Was there one word, one moment, one gesture, one day when things started to change? Will I ever get over this?

Today I...

As the girls get excited with the things they have accomplished they set up the table, four chairs and three martinis for the next scene.

A: Today, I found the nape of another man's neck sexy.

C: Today, I woke up before my alarm clock.

B: Today, I realized that I don't want to understand football.

A: Today, I bought my own garlic press.

C: Today, I shaved my legs.

B: Today, I took him off my speed dial.

A: Today, I didn't drive past his house once!

B: Today, I only read my horoscope.

C: Today, I had a…

B: …martini at

A: …Franco's.

The girls toast each other and sit down and cross their legs simultaneously, as in the first scene.

Return to Franco's

The three women are once again in the café from the opening scene. D runs in, notices them out of the corner of his eye and turns to avoid them, but they have seen him.

A,B,C: Hi!

D: Oh, hi. How are you?

A: Busy.

B: Fine.

C: OK.

A: *(To B and C.)* Smile, be funny.

B: *(To A and C.)* Don't cry, don't cry, don't cry.

C: *(To A and B who do the actions as she says.)* Sit up straight, suck in stomach, make arms look thin.

D: You look great.

A: I feel great.

B: Really?

C: Yeah.

B: So

C: do

A: you.

> *They gesture for him to sit down. The following lines are repeated three times simultaneously.*

A: He's got a paunch!

B: Has he always had a monobrow?

C: He looks like a lizard.

A,B,C: So…

B: how

C: are

A: you?

D: *(As he speaks the three women nod their heads to the rhythm of his speech.)* Busy. Good. Good busy.

A: So much for slowing down,

B: listening,

C: being alone.

D: Sorry?

A,B,C: Nothing…

A: I am Wonder Woman, Joan of Arc. *(She does a superhero gesture.)*

B: *(Singing dreamily.)* "Somewhere over the rainbow…"

C: *(With great conviction.)* "I am a rock, I am an island."

A: So how's the band?

D: What?

B: So, did you get your magic back?

D: Uh, ye...I ...uh...yeah.

C: So can we talk about daycare?

D: Uh, I'll call you.

A, B, and C lean back in their chairs.

A: Wow.

C: Wow.

B: Wow.

A: I am

C: over

B: him.

A: Franco arrives

B: with another

C: martini.

A,B,C: Hey Franco. *(They smile sweetly and wave.)*

D turns around and realizes that Franco no longer wants him in his restaurant.

D: I should...

A,B,C: Yeah, you should...

D: ...go. I'll call you.

A,B,C: No.

B: I'll

C: call

A: you.

B: Bye.

C: Bye.

A: Bye.

> *The three women wave at him and in turn breathe a huge sigh.*

Bittergirl Manifesto

> *They stand up and make a singing trio formation, with B in the middle and A and C flanked on either side as the back up singers. Throughout the final scene A and C perform corresponding gestures to their lines as B reaches out to the audience with their message.*

B: Everyone has their war story.

C: Joe. Wouldn't let me eat in his car.

B: Some have many stories.

A: Fraser. Wore tighty whities.

B: But there's always one.

C: Patrick. Wore white tube socks. With black dress shoes.

B: The one that we coin the breakup of all breakups.

A: Ken. The couples therapist with commitment issues.

B: And everyone thinks that their story is the most painful.

C: Brian. Gave me shoelaces for my birthday.

B: "Nobody hurt like I did," we say.

A: Geoffrey. Growled during sex.

B: We thrive on it, we bond through it.

C: Buzz. The name kinda says it all.

B: Yet if someone takes our glory, if someone's story surpasses the pain and hurt of our tale, we dismiss it.

A: Paul. Told me I was selfish in bed.

B: Don't dismiss it.

C: George. Stopped calling...

C,A: ...and I never noticed.

B: We've all earned our scars.

A: Matt. Cried at Celine Dion songs.

B: But remember, when all hope is lost...

C: Blake. Wouldn't memorize my phone number.

B: When you feel there's no tomorrow...

A: John. Asked if a "pickle wash" would be out of the question.

B: You're walking in darkness and drowning in sorrow...

C: Bobby. Whispered "Baby have I got a load for you."

B: Remember...

A: Gary. Had middle child issues.

B: Yesterday's heartache is tomorrow's one liner.

C: Rick. Referred to my legs as nutcrackers.

B:	That's what we do. It's how we get through.

A:	I've got

B:	my

C:	story—

A,B,C:	What's yours?

The End.